# Olympic Sports

**Nick Hunter**

**WAYLAND**

First published in 2011 by Wayland

Copyright © Wayland 2011

Wayland
338 Euston Road
London NW1 3BH

Wayland Australia
Level 17/207 Kent Street
Sydney, NSW 2000

Produced for Wayland by Calcium
Design: Simon Borrough and Paul Myerscough
Editor: Sarah Eason
Editor for Wayland: Katie Woolley
Picture researcher: Susannah Jayes

British Library Cataloguing in Publication Data

Hunter, Nick.
   Olympic sports.—(The Olympics)
   1. Olympic Games (30th : 2012 : London, England)—
   Juvenile literature. 2. Sports—Juvenile literature.
   I. Title II. Series
   796.4'8-dc22

ISBN: 978 0 7502 6436 5

Printed in China
Wayland is a division of Hachette Children's Books,
an Hachette UK company.
www.hachette.co.uk

Picture Acknowledgements:

**Cover** Main image: Shutterstock: Jamie Roach. Inset
images: Shutterstock: John Lumb tl, Muzsy tr, Chad
McDermott bl, Pete Niesen br. Spine image:
Shutterstock: Herbert Kratky. Back cover image:
Shutterstock: Peter Kirillov.
**Pages** Corbis: Jens Buettner/EPA 13b, Fabrice Coffrini/
EPA 6, Kimimasa Mayama/Reuters 14, Reix-Liewig/For
Pictures 4, Zhang Chen/xh/Xinhua Press 25tr; Dreamstime:
Bedo 23tl, Fstockfoto 21br, Pniesen 7, Nadiya Vlashchenko
28; Getty Images: 18, AFP 9, 17, 20; London 2012: 5,
28-29; PA Photos: 23br; Shutterstock: Galina Barskaya
15tr, Olga Besnard 24, Vince Clements 19, Chris Curtis
10, Adam Fraise 21tr, Fstockfoto 11tr, 22, 25bl, 26, 27,
Herbert Kratky 1, PhotoStock10 15bl, Chen Wei Seng
29, Sportgraphic 11bl, 13tr, Sportsphotographer.eu 8,
Webitect 2, 16, Vladimir Wrangel 12.

# Contents

# The world watches

It is late July 2012. At different **venues** across London and the rest of the United Kingdom, spectators are watching as some of the world's greatest athletes take the stage. At the Velodrome, track cyclists are racing wheel to wheel. In the table tennis arena, fans are amazed by the players' lightning-fast reflexes. Cheering crowds applaud the performances, from the athletes in the Olympic Stadium to the beach volleyball players at Horse Guards Parade.

Jamaican sprinter Usain Bolt took the gold medal in the men's 200-metre race at the 2008 Games in Beijing, and he is a hot favourite to win again in 2012.

### Olympic insights

Some unusual events have been part of the Olympics throughout history. In 1904, the 'plunge for distance' was part of the St Louis Olympics. Competitors dived into a pool and stayed motionless. The athlete who dived the furthest and remained under water the longest was the winner.

## The Olympic story

Olympic history goes back thousands of years to ancient Greece, where the first Games were held in 776 BCE. The first Olympics included only a single running race, but it wasn't long before other sports were added. The Games died out with the ancient Greeks in 349 CE, but were brought to life once more in 1896, when the first 'modern' Olympic Games were held in Athens, Greece. Then it was decided that, as well as the Summer Olympics, a Winter Olympics for snow and ice sports would be held. It was first staged in 1924 in Chamonix, France. Then, in 1960 in Rome, Italy, the first **Paralympics** for athletes with disabilities took place.

## London's turn

Today, the Summer Olympics are held every four years by a **host** country. The Winter Olympics take place two years after the Summer Olympics. In 2012, the world will look to London, the next Summer Olympic host city. There, people will see a wide range of sports – some can trace their **origins** back to the ancient Games, but there are plenty of exciting 'modern-day' sports too, including BMX racing, basketball, shooting and sailing.

### Olympics by numbers
There will be **26** different sports at the London Olympics in 2012 and **300** separate events. Athletics awards gold medals in **47** events and swimming has **34** different events.

In 2012, London will put on the greatest sporting show on Earth. Many events will take place in the Olympic Stadium.

# On your marks

For many spectators, events on the athletics track in the Olympic Stadium are what the Games are all about. Whether they are sprinting or running long distance races, all track athletes need stamina, speed, strength and clear tactics to win.

## What makes a great sprinter?

Sprint races are all about power and pace as races are often decided by fractions of a second. A fast start is essential and by pushing off starting blocks, runners can get away quickly. New materials have made it possible to create lighter running shoes and rubberised race tracks that can stop runners slipping – helping them gain those extra few hundredths of a second. Sprint **hurdlers** must also combine the pace of a sprinter with great jumping techniques to clear 10 hurdles during the race.

### Olympic insights

A runner has finished when his or her torso, from shoulder to waist, crosses the finish line. In a close race, sprinters lean forwards, or dip, at the finish to get a little extra advantage.

In the 100-metre race at the Athens Games in 2004, US sprinter Justin Gatlin (right) crossed the line first to take the gold medal.
Portugal's Francis Obikwelu (second from left) dipped to take the silver.

## Tactical racing

Track races are not just for sprinters. Races are also run at 400, 800, 1,500, 5,000 and 10,000 metres. The 3,000-metre **steeplechase** includes hurdles and a jump over water.

Many of the most amazing Olympic performances have been in long-distance competitions, in which African athletes have dominated recent Olympics. Ethiopian greats, Tirunesh Dibaba (female) and Kenenisa Bekele (male) won two gold medals each at the 5,000- and 10,000-metre races in Beijing.

Kenyan Brimin Kipruto (centre) took the gold medal in the 3,000-metre steeplechase at the 2008 Games in Beijing.

### Olympics by numbers
*Here are some of the greatest athletics wins:*

**100 metres – Women**
Florence Griffith-Joyner (USA), **10.62** seconds (1988)

**400 metres – Men**
Michael Johnson (USA), **43.49** seconds (1996)

**400 metres – Women**
Marie-José Pérec (France), **48.25** seconds (1996)

**1,500 metres – Men**
Noah Ngeny (Kenya), **3** minutes, **32.07** seconds (2000)

**10,000 metres – Men**
Kenenisa Bekele (Ethiopia), **27** minutes, **01.17** seconds (2008)

**100 metres – Men**
Usain Bolt (Jamaica), **9.69** seconds (2008)

**10,000 metres – Women**
Tirunesh Dibaba (Ethiopia), **29** minutes, **54.66** seconds (2008)

> " When anyone tells me I can't do anything, I'm just not listening anymore. "
> Florence Griffith-Joyner, 1988 100-metre sprint gold medallist.

# Jumping and throwing

Athletics also features field events, including long jump, triple jump, high jump and throwing contests, such as **shot put**, **javelin** and **discus**. The Olympic motto is 'Faster, Higher, Stronger' and athletes must be all three to triumph in field events.

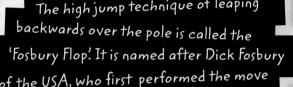

The high jump technique of leaping backwards over the pole is called the 'Fosbury Flop'. It is named after Dick Fosbury of the USA, who first performed the move at the 1968 Olympics, where he took the gold medal.

## Leaping for gold

In high jump and pole vault, athletes must clear a horizontal bar without touching it. High jumpers leap backwards over the bar to land on their backs. Pole vaulters use a long pole to propel themselves high into the air and over the bar. They must have great upper body strength and agility to jump heights of more than five metres. In long jump and triple jump, athletes take a run-up before jumping as far as possible into a sand pit.

## Strength and technique

Olympic throwing events include the **hammer**, shot put, discus and javelin competitions. While each sport requires upper body strength, technique is just as important. Hammer and discus athletes spin around to give their throws added force. Athletes must aim precisely and release the ball at exactly the right moment to ensure a successful throw.

The shot put competition has been an Olympic event since its first appearance at the 1912 Games.

### Olympic insights

Javelin and discus throwing were both part of the ancient Olympic Games. Like many ancient Olympic sports, javelin throwing was part of the training for ancient Greek soldiers. The hammer throw has its origins in **sledgehammer** throwing in sixteenth century Scotland and England.

# All-round athletes

Some of the toughest competitors at the Olympics are all-round athletes who take part in events such as the triathlon, decathlon and heptathlon. These challenging competitions require participants to complete several gruelling events, in which they must demonstrate athletic skills including running, jumping, cycling and throwing.

Road cycling is one of three categories that make up the triathlon event. The other categories are swimming and running.

### Olympic insights
Only a few athletes have won medals at both Summer and Winter Olympics. Edward Eagan (USA) won gold in both boxing (1920 Summer Olympics) and **bobsleigh** (1932 Winter Olympics). More recently, Canada's Clara Hughes won two bronze medals in cycling in 1996 and has won four speed skating medals at three Winter Olympics in 2002, 2006 and 2010.

## Ancient all-rounders

All-round athletes were revered at the ancient Olympics in Greece. The greatest Olympic champion was the winner of the pentathlon, which included a running race, discus and javelin throws, long jump and wrestling. Today, the 'modern' pentathlon includes different sports such as fencing and shooting. The triathlon was introduced to the Olympics in 2000 and in 2012, the triathlon will be held in London's Hyde Park, with the swimming stage taking place in the park's Serpentine Lake.

The 'modern' pentathlon includes five events: fencing (above), horse riding, running, swimming and shooting.

## WORD FILE

**decathlon event (men):** features ten sports over two days. A 100-metre sprint, long jump, shot put, high jump and 400-metre race make up day one. Day two includes 110-metre hurdles, discus, pole vault, javelin and the final 1,500-metre race

**heptathlon event (women):** features seven sports over two days. Day one includes 100-metre hurdles, high jump, shot put and a 200-metre sprint. Day two sports are long jump, javelin and the 800-metre race

Long jumpers extend their legs and push their torso forwards to gain the maximum distance in their jump.

11

# Endurance athletes

Many sports test athletes' stamina, from rowing and road cycling to the marathon and the 10-kilometre swim. To be successful, athletes in endurance events must be able to maintain high energy levels over long periods of time by eating a high-energy diet and improving their stamina through training. On average, endurance athletes spend six hours a day training to achieve the fitness levels required to compete in an Olympic event.

Rowing uses more muscle groups than almost any other sport as the athletes push themselves to 40 or 45 oar strokes per minute.

## WORD FILE

*Key rowing terms and their meanings:*

**bow:** *front section of a boat or shell*

**coxswain or cox:** *person who sits at the stern of the boat during some rowing races to steer and direct the rowers*

**full paddle:** *rowing as fast as possible*

**sculls:** *rowing with two oars per person. Sculls events can include one, two or four people*

**shell:** *rowing boat for racing, made of wood or* **carbon fibre**

**sweep:** *rowing with one oar. Sweep rowers race in teams of two, four or eight*

# Longest Olympic races

Cycling road races are long, tactical battles. The men's road race is 250 kilometres (180 miles) long, while the women compete over 140 kilometres (86 miles). Near the finish line, the fastest sprinters break away from the pack and try to win the race.

The marathon is the toughest running race at the Olympics – runners must run for 42.195 kilometres (26.2 miles), often covering each mile in just under five minutes. The event has been part of the Games since 1896, although a women's marathon race was not added until 1984 after many years of campaigning by female runners to persuade the **International Olympic Committee** (IOC) to add the event to the Olympic programme. The longest race on foot is not the marathon, but the 50-kilometre race walk, which takes around three and a half hours. Walkers must keep one foot on the ground at all times and straighten their front leg as it hits the ground.

During a road race, cyclists bunch together in a 'pack' called a peloton.

## Olympic insights

Rowers need between 4,000 and 6,000 calories per day when training. That's more than twice the amount most adults should eat. It can be difficult to eat this much, so endurance athletes must eat foods that are easily digestible but high in energy, such as rice and pasta.

Samuel Wanjiru set a new world record by completing the Beijing Olympic marathon in two hours, six minutes and 32 seconds.

# Gymnastics

The O2 was built for London's Millennium celebrations in 2000 and has since become a successful concert venue. In 2012, crowds will be thrilled by the grace and strength of the world's gymnasts as this arena hosts the Olympic gymnastic and trampolining competitions.

## Olympic bounce

Trampolining is the newest sport in Olympic gymnastics, making its debut at the Sydney Games in 2000. Gymnasts perform a series of short routines, which contain a variety of twists, bounces and somersaults.

Competitors must display precise technique and perfect body control throughout their performance. Judges award points for the difficulty of the routine, the skill with which moves such as somersaults are performed and the height of the jumps achieved. Top gymnasts can reach heights of 10 metres!

### Olympic insights
American George Eyser won three gold medals for gymnastics at the 1904 Olympics in St Louis, USA, which was amazing enough in itself. Even more remarkably, Eyser's left leg was made of wood. He had lost his leg after he was run over by a train.

In 2004, Anna Dogonadze of Germany won the gold medal in the women's trampolining competition in Athens.

## Grace under pressure

Women's gymnastics includes combined team and individual events in four different disciplines: beam, floor exercises, uneven bars and vault. Men's gymnastics includes different disciplines, such as rings and the pommel horse, which need great upper body strength. Gymnastic competitions are marked by two panels of judges: one panel decides on the difficulty of the routine and the other marks the quality of the gymnast's performance.

Male gymnasts perform swings, handstands and strength moves (in which the body is held perfectly still) on rings elevated nine metres above the ground.

### Olympics by numbers

Gymnast Larisa Latynina has won more Olympic medals than any other athlete. Between 1956 and 1964, the gymnast from Ukraine, then part of the USSR, won **18** medals including nine golds. It is possible that US swimmer Michael Phelps, who has already won **16** medals, may surpass Latynina's amazing record in 2012.

Rhythmic gymnastics, in which competitors perform floor routines using equipment such as ribbons and balls, also feature in Olympic gymnastics.

15

# In the pool

Around 1,450 athletes will take part in the **aquatics** competitions in 2012. Each separate sport in the pool tests different skills, from the power and technique of swimming and water polo to the skill and precision of diving and synchronised swimming.

## Olympic insights

*Olympic swimming venues were fairly basic in times gone by. At the 1900 Paris Olympics, competitions were held in the River Seine and the pool at London's first Olympics in 1908 was in the middle of the Olympic Stadium's running track! The brand new Aquatics Centre in London's Olympic Park has come a long way since then.*

## Swimming

There are four main disciplines in swimming: freestyle, backstroke, breaststroke and butterfly. Swimmers compete at distances of up to 1,500 metres. The 10-kilometre marathon swim, which takes place in open water, was added to the Olympic programme at the Beijing Olympics in 2008. The women's open water event was won by Russian swimmer Larisa Ilchenko in one hour, 59 minutes and 27.7 seconds. The men's event was won by the Netherlands swimmer Maarten van der Weijden, who finished the race with a speed of one hour, 51 minutes and 51.6 seconds.

US swimmer Natalie Coughlin competed in six events at the 2008 Games, and won a medal in each! She is currently in training for the 2012 Games.

## Daring divers

In the platform event, divers try to complete complex dives that include difficult moves, such as somersaults and twists. Dives are made from a diving board positioned 10 metres above the pool's surface. Judges award points for each dive, which are adjusted depending on the difficulty of the move. Points are also awarded for the diver's take-off from the diving board, the control displayed as the diver carries out the move and how 'clean' his or her entry into the water is.

Tom Daley, the British diver, hopes to win gold at the 2012 Games. At just 14 years old, he was the youngest competitor of any sport at the 2008 Olympics.

## Diving together

Synchronised diving events were added to the Olympic programme in 2000. In this event two competitors from the same team perform a dive at the same time, while trying to perfectly mirror each other's movements.

"My dream is a gold... with a lot of work...I hope to achieve that. Tom Daley, speaking about his hopes for the Olympics in 2012.

## WORD FILE

Key diving terms and their meanings:

**arm stand:** platform dive that begins from a handstand position

**pike:** body position with hips bent and legs straight

**springboard:** event using a long board three metres above the pool

**tuck:** position with hips and legs bent and pulled close to the body

# On the water

Most of the events on water at the 2012 Olympics will take place outside the capital. Rowing and canoe sprint events will be staged at Eton Dorney near Windsor. A specially designed **white-water** course has been built at the Lee Valley White Water Centre in Hertfordshire for canoe slalom. Sailing events will be held at Weymouth and Portland on the south coast.

## Sailing at the Olympics

There will be 10 gold medals awarded for sailing at the London Olympics. Today's sailing competitions use small, light boats with no more than three people on board. Each crew member can directly affect the balance and performance of the boat, making sailing a test of the agility and skill of each athlete. Sailors must position their bodies and the boat's sails perfectly to balance the vessel and to make use of the wind.

**Olympic insights**
Great Britain has been the most successful sailing nation in the last three Olympics. Ben Ainslie has won gold medals at each Games since Sydney in 2000, and the British team won three gold medals in 2008.

In the laser class sailing event, each small dinghy is manned by just one sailor.

## White-water winners

Canoes and kayaks used in canoe slalom are small and light to make it easier for athletes to guide them around poles, called gates, on a challenging white-water course. Athletes race against the clock and there are time penalties for touching or missing a gate. In canoe sprint races, individuals or teams of two or four paddlers race each other over distances of up to 1,000 metres on a straight course.

In the white-water canoe slalom event, athletes must navigate a 300-metre course without touching the gates.

# WORD FILE

*Key sailing terms and their meanings:*

**class:** *the model of boat. Olympic sailors race against each other in the same class of boats*

**dinghy:** *small sailing boat*

**fleet racing:** *style of race used at the Olympics when all the competitors race against each other*

**match racing:** *style of race in which one boat races against another. Match racing will feature in the women's competition in 2012*

**trapese:** *harness fitted to the mast of a boat so sailors can safely put all their weight over the side of the boat*

# Combat sports

Many of the **combat sports** at the Olympics have ancient origins. Boxing and wrestling were part of the ancient Games in Greece and will still feature in London in 2012. Fencing developed from **swordsmanship**, and evidence has been found that indicates sword fighting was a sport in many ancient cultures, including the gladiator swordfights in ancient Roman arenas.

Taekwondo is practised by 60 million people worldwide. Afghan Rohullah Nikpai (above left) won his country's first Olympic medal when he took the bronze in 2008.

## Punching and kicking

Taekwondo means 'the art of punching and kicking' in Korean. As the name suggests, each taekwonda (athlete) tries to hit an opponent with the hands or feet. The sport developed from several ancient combat techniques going back more than 2,000 years, although the name taekwondo was only given to the sport in the 1950s.

## The gentle way

Judo means 'gentle way' in Japanese. The aim of judo is to score an 'ippon', meaning 'one full point'. This can be achieved by throwing the opponent onto their back and keeping them under control by pinning them down on the floor for 30 seconds.

The main principle of judo is that a competitor does not resist, but turns the opponent's force against him.

## WORD FILE

Key judo terms and their meanings:

**judogi:** white or blue cotton jacket and trousers worn for judo

**judoka:** an expert or competitor in judo

**matte:** shouted by the referee to interrupt a fight. Athletes must separate when hearing this

**tatami:** mat that is used for a judo contest

## In the ring

Originally **professional** athletes were not allowed to compete at the Olympics, and while this has changed for many sports, just **amateurs** are still only allowed to compete in Olympic boxing events because its rules are very different from those of professional boxing. Like most combat sports at the Olympics, boxers are divided into different weight divisions so that athletes compete against others of a similar size. Olympic boxers win a point for each punch they land on their opponent's head or upper body. Each match is made up of four rounds lasting two minutes.

Boxing was once a male-only event at the Olympics, but in 2012 women's boxing will feature for the first time.

# Team sports

Many Olympic sports rely on teamwork just as much as individual brilliance to win medals. Team athletes range from amateur hockey and handball players to high-profile football stars and basketball teams. Sports such as basketball have become popular since professionals have been allowed to compete at the Olympics, and huge crowds gather at the Games to see top players in action.

## Olympic football

Men's football at the Olympics is a competition for players under the age of 23. Each team is also allowed to include three players over that age. The last two Olympic men's tournaments have been won by Argentina, with young stars including Carlos Tevez and Lionel Messi in the team. Women's football has no age limits. The USA has won three gold medals since women's football was first played at the Olympics in 1996.

## Cycling teams

Both road and track cycling will be 2012 events. British stars such as Chris Hoy and Victoria Pendleton will be hoping to continue their dominance of track cycling at the London Olympics. To do this, they will have to work as teams in events including the team sprint and team pursuit, in which each cyclist in the team takes a turn leading the race to save the energy of other team members.

Football star Ronaldinho celebrates a goal against New Zealand with other members of the Brazilian team at the 2008 Games.

## Horse and rider

All **equestrian** events are for teams of horses and their riders. As well as individual medals, there are medals for the best teams of three horses and riders from each nation. In the three equestrian sports of dressage, jumping and eventing both men and women compete against each other. In dressage, horses are tested on movements such as the piaffe (trotting on the spot) and the half-pass (moving forwards and sideways at the same time).

Eventing includes **dressage**, jumping (shown above) and cross-country riding.

### Olympics by numbers

From 1936, when basketball first appeared at the Olympics, the USA won **62** games in a row before losing in the final in 1972. In 1992, professional NBA stars appeared at the Olympics for the first time. The US 'Dream Team' averaged **117** points per game and won all their games by more than **30** points, taking the gold medal.

The US basketball team claimed gold once more at the 2008 Olympics, and are the strong favourite to win again at the 2012 Games.

23

# What a racket!

The Olympic tennis champions in 2012 will be crowned on Wimbledon's Centre Court. Rafael Nadal will have to work hard to defend the title he won in 2008 as stars such as Roger Federer and Andy Murray will play a tough game, knowing that the chance to be an Olympic champion only comes every four years. The Williams sisters will probably be the team to beat in the women's doubles and the 2012 Games will also feature mixed doubles for the first time since 1924.

## Olympics by numbers

Racket sports players need amazingly fast reactions. A table tennis ball travels at **160** kilometres per hour. The fastest servers in tennis can send the ball across the net at more than **225** kilometres per hour. A badminton shuttlecock can travel at more than **300** kilometres per hour.

## Fast and furious

Tennis is not the only Olympic racket sport. Badminton matches are fast and exciting, with players hitting the shuttlecock as hard as possible to force the opposition to make a mistake.

Doubles competitions are even quicker than singles matches because players do not have to move as far to return the shuttlecock. The shuttlecock is made of cork surrounded by 16 feathers from the left wing of a goose. It has to stay in the air at all times. Points are won if players can hit the shuttlecock onto the ground on their opponent's side of the net.

Elena Dementieva won gold at the 2008 Beijing Olympics. The Russian star player has since retired and will not make an appearance at the 2012 Games.

Table tennis, like badminton, is dominated by players from Asian countries including China, where it is a massively popular sport. It became an Olympic sport in 1988. The game moves very fast so it is easy to miss the techniques that top competitors use to try to outwit their opponents, such as spins and lobs.

Badminton star Lin Dan of China was overjoyed to win gold at the 2008 Games in his home country.

## Olympic insights

Table tennis originated in the UK during the 1880s, where it was an after-dinner pastime in wealthy households. It has since become an international sport that is now dominated by China, the hot favourites to take home the gold in 2012.

Ryu Seung Min (top) brought victory to South Korea when he took the table tennis gold at the 2004 Games in Athens. It was the first time since 1992 that the gold medallist had not been Chinese.

# Winter sports

The sports that make up the Summer Olympics are really only part of the Olympic story. Winter sports such as **figure skating** and ice hockey were included in the Summer Olympics in 1920, but then became features of the Winter Games in 1924. The next Winter Olympics will be held in Sochi, Russia, in 2014.

## High-speed sports

All sports at the Winter Olympics take place on snow or ice. Sliding sports such as bobsleigh, luge and skeleton are the fastest sports at the Winter or Summer Olympics, with athletes hurtling down a sheet of ice at around 145 kilometres per hour. At 130 kilometres per hour, Olympic downhill skiers travel almost as fast.

Olympic bobsleigh teams can be made up of a four-person crew (above) or a two-person crew. Each team competes to achieve the fastest speed as they slide down a track of ice.

### Olympics by numbers

The Vancouver Winter Olympics in 2010 welcomed **2,566** athletes from **82** countries. They competed in **86** events across **15** sports.

## Skating stars

Figure skaters showcase dazzling routines on ice. Skaters perform to music and include challenging moves such as jumps and spins in their routines. Skaters are judged on the complexity of their moves and the skill with which they perform their routine. Speed skating is a high-speed race in which racers can reach speeds of 95 kilometres per hour.

In ice hockey, players aim to hit a rubber **puck** into the opposing team's goal. Players use shoulders and hips to tackle opponents as they try to gain control of the puck.

Speed skaters wear **aerodynamic** body suits that keep them warm while allowing them to move freely on the ice.

## WORD FILE

*Key Winter Olympic sports:*

***biathlon:*** *sport that combines cross-country skiing with shooting*

***curling:*** *sport in which two teams slide 'stones' or rocks along the ice towards a target*

***luge:*** *sliding event in which one or two athletes lie on their backs on a sled*

***skeleton:*** *sliding event in which one athlete lies face-down on a sled and slides down a track of ice*

## New sports

The Winter Olympics have also been quick to take in newer sports such as snowboarding and **freestyle skiing**. New events at the Vancouver Winter Olympics in 2010 included ski cross, in which skiers raced against each other over a twisting course with bumps and jumps. New events at the 2014 Winter Olympics in Russia will include **ski halfpipe**, **biathlon** mixed relay and a figure skating team event.

# Changing Olympic sports

There were nine sports at the first 'modern' Olympic Games in 1896. Some sports, such as athletics, swimming and fencing, have been part of the Games ever since. Many new sports have been added and removed as the Olympic Games have become a global event, culminating in a huge variety of sports that will feature in London in 2012.

Sports can be dropped from the Olympic programme. Baseball and softball were the most recent sports to be removed after the 2008 Olympics. The IOC, which decides which sports should be part of the Games, felt that these sports did not have enough worldwide appeal.

### Olympic insights

Some unusual sports were part of the Olympics in the past, such as tug-of-war, Jeu de Paume (also called **real tennis**) and motorboating. All are no longer featured in the Games. Squash, karate and roller sports (such as roller skating) failed in their bid to become Olympic sports in 2016, but golf and rugby sevens were successful and will feature at the 2016 Games in Rio de Janeiro.

Rugby sevens is played by seven members in each team. Matches are made of two halves, with each lasting 10 minutes.

## Sports for everyone

The **Olympic Movement** continually reviews the many sports featured at the Olympics, and updates its programme to include new sports. BMX and mountain biking became Olympic sports in 2008. These sports developed during the 1970s and 1980s as bikes became light and tough enough to race across rough terrain.

## Paralympics

Just a few weeks after the Olympics, athletes with disabilities will meet in London for the 2012 Paralympics. Athletes with disabilities will take part in 20 different sports using the same sporting venues as the Olympics. Many of these sports, such as wheelchair athletics or cycling for the **visually-impaired**, are adapted versions of Olympic sports.

Visually-impaired runners race with a sighted guide companion. The two runners hold a tie that joins them during the race.

# Olympic trivia

Discover some amazing facts and figures about the Olympics.

At the first 'modern' Olympic Games in Athens in 1896, silver medals were awarded to the winners.

Athletes at the ancient Olympics in Greece competed naked.

More athletes than spectators attended the 1900 Olympics in Paris.

Women were first allowed to compete at the Olympics in the 1900 Games.

The oldest person to ever compete at the Olympics was Oscar Swahn, a Swedish shooter. He won his sixth Olympic medal at the 1920 Games in Antwerp, Belgium, when he was 72 years old!

The youngest person to ever compete at the Olympics was 10-year-old Greek gymnast Dimitrios Loundras. He competed in the 1896 Olympics in Athens.

Men and women compete against each other in only two Olympic sports – sailing and equestrian events.

Pigeon shooting was once an Olympic sport.

The medals for the 2008 Beijing Games were inlaid with a piece of jade. In Chinese culture, jade represents beauty and excellence in all things.

Between 1900–1920, the Olympics included a tug-of-war event.

The design of the Olympic flag, with five rings, was created by Pierre de Coubertin in 1914.

# Glossary

**aerodynamic** designed to move through air with maximum speed

**amateurs** people who are not paid for what they do

**aquatics** sports that take place in water, such as swimming and diving

**biathlon** a sporting competition made up of two events

**bobsleigh** a sport in which teams of two or four people travel down an ice track in a sled-like vehicle

**carbon fibre** light, strong material

**combat sports** sports where athletes simulate combat. Many of these sports had their origins in training for soldiers

**discus** an event in which a metal disc is thrown as far as possible

**dressage** an equestrian event (see below) in which horses perform movements such as trotting on the spot

**equestrian** relating to horses

**figure skating** performing ice skating routines with moves such as jumps

**freestyle skiing** a form of skiing in which skiers ski down a ramp and jump into the air, where they perform acrobatic moves such as spins

**hammer** an event in which a heavy ball attached to a wire and handle is thrown

**host** to stage or organise an event

**hurdlers** runners that also jump over fences called hurdles during the race

**International Olympic Committee** the organisation that leads the Olympic Movement and oversees the organisation of the Olympic Games

**javelin** an event in which a spear-like object called a javelin is thrown as far as possible

**Olympic Movement** the name for all the groups involved in planning the Olympics

**origins** beginnings, such as when and where a sport was first played

**Paralympics** a sporting event for athletes with disabilities

**professional** someone who is paid for what they do

**puck** a small, round object that is hit into a net to score a goal

**real tennis** the original form of tennis (once called royal tennis) that was played by kings such as Henry VIII

**shot put** an event in which a heavy metal ball is thrown as far as possible

**ski halfpipe** an event in which skiers ski down a U-shaped ramp and perform tricks in the air at each end

**sledgehammer** a very large hammer with a heavy metal or wooden head

**steeplechase** a hurdle event in which athletes race over hurdles that include water jumps

**swordsmanship** skill with a sword

**venues** buildings or locations where something happens. Each Olympic sport takes place in a particular venue

**visually-impaired** a disability affecting the eyes and a person's ability to see

**white-water** water flowing over rocks and obstacles to create a course for canoe slalom

# Further information

## Books

*British Olympians (21st Century Lives)*
by Debbie Foy (Wayland, 2009)

*Cycling (Olympic Sports)*
by Clive Gifford (Franklin Watts, 2011)

*High-Tech Olympics (Olympics)*
by Nick Hunter (Raintree, 2011)

*Improving Speed (Training for Sport)*
by Paul Mason (Wayland, 2010)

## Websites

Find out more about Olympic sports, athletes and records by exploring the world governing body for athletics at:
**www.iaaf.org**

For information about swimming and other aquatic sports, visit the world governing body for water sports at:
**www.fina.org**

Visit the official 2012 Olympic websites:
**www.london2012.com/sports**
**www.olympic.org/sports**

# Index

# Contents of titles in the series:

## Behind the Scenes at the Olympics

ISBN: 978 0 7502 6595 9

The world's greatest
    sporting event
The Olympic Movement
The winning bid
Staging the Games
Building the venues
Beyond the Olympic Park
Symbols and ceremonies
Olympic sports
The athletes
Paralympic dreams
Science at the Olympics
Media and merchandise
After the Games
Countdown to London

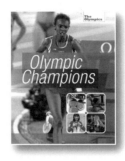

## Olympic Champions

ISBN: 978 0 7502 6596 6

In pursuit of gold
Lightning fast: Usain Bolt
The all-rounder: Jessica Ennis
Long-distance legend:
    Tirunesh Dibaba
Cycling star: Victoria Pendleton
Golden rower: Tom James
Tennis ace: Rafael Nadal
Badminton's best: Lin Dan
Top triathlete: Emma Snowsill
Young diving star: Tom Daley
Swimming superstars
Stars of the future
True champions
Olympic gold

## Olympic Sports

ISBN: 978 0 7502 6436 5

The world watches
On your marks
Jumping and throwing
All-round athletes
Endurance athletes
Gymnastics
In the pool
On the water
Combat sports
Team sports
What a racket!
Winter sports
Changing Olympic sports
Olympic trivia

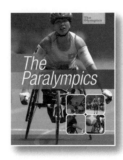

## The Paralympics

ISBN: 978 0 7502 6597 3

Paralympics 2012
How the Paralympics began
The Paralympics Movement
Making the Paralympics
    happen
Paralympic athletes
Track and field
Paralympic swimming
Cycle racers
Team sports
Venues and sports
Winter Paralympics
Paralympic controversies
The London Paralympics
Paralympic legends